Bird Watching
For
Couples

PARADOX
PRESS

Bird Watching Log Book

Name:	
Start Date:	
Address:	
Email:	
Contact:	

INDEX		
Page	Date	Sightings

INDEX		
Page	Date	Sightings

INDEX		
Page	Date	Sightings

INDEX		
Page	Date	Sightings

Page	Date	Sightings

INDEX		
Page	Date	Sightings

Page	Date	Sightings

INDEX		
Page	Date	Sightings

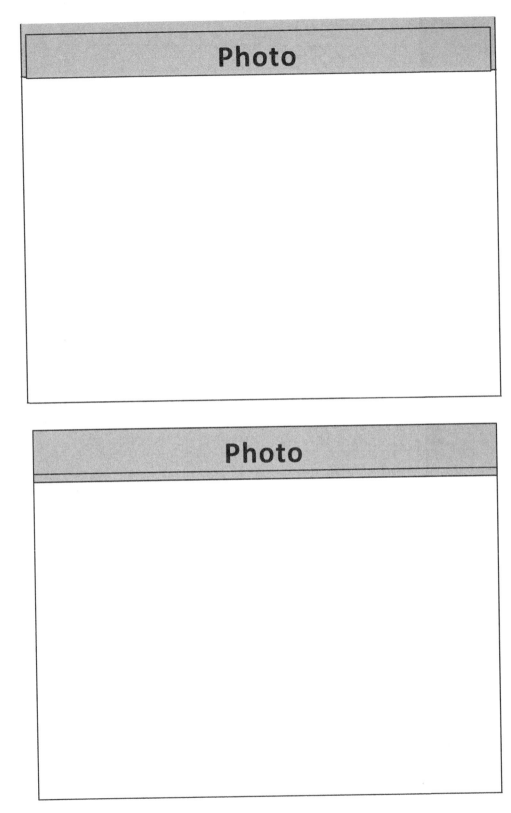

Date:	
Weather:	
Season:	
Location:	

Bird Sighting	
Bird Species:	
Time Seen:	
Markings:	

Description

Notes/Remarks

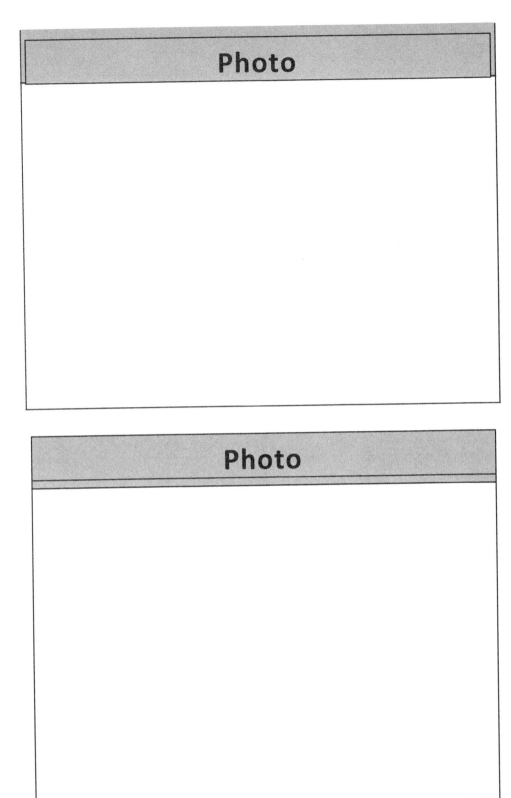

Photo

Photo

Date:	
Weather:	
Season:	
Location:	

Bird Sighting

Bird Species:	
Time Seen:	
Markings:	

Description

Notes/Remarks

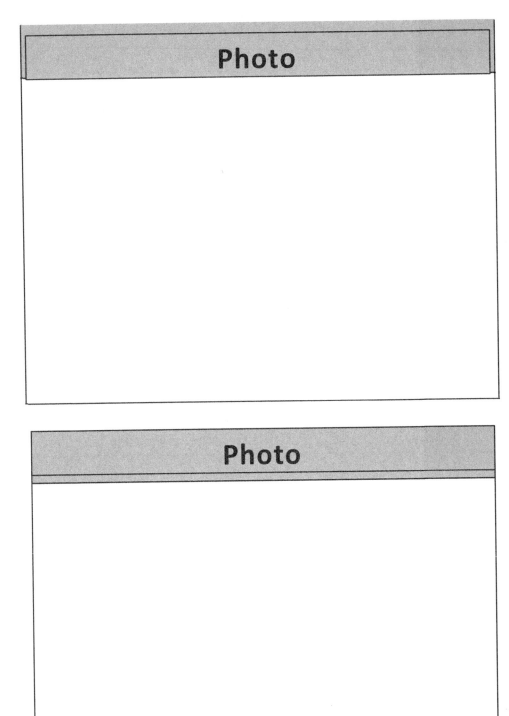

Photo

Photo

Date:	
Weather:	
Season:	
Location:	

Bird Sighting

Bird Species:	
Time Seen:	
Markings:	

Description

Notes/Remarks

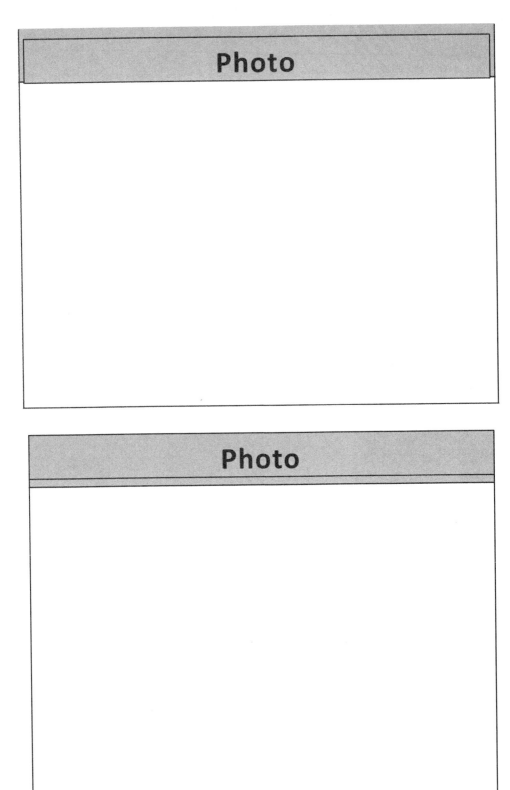

Photo

Photo

Date:	
Weather:	
Season:	
Location:	

Bird Sighting	
Bird Species:	
Time Seen:	
Markings:	

Description

Notes/Remarks

Photo

Photo

Date:	
Weather:	
Season:	
Location:	

Bird Sighting

Bird Species:	
Time Seen:	
Markings:	

Description

Notes/Remarks

Photo

Photo

Date:	
Weather:	
Season:	
Location:	

Bird Sighting

Bird Species:	
Time Seen:	
Markings:	

Description

Notes/Remarks

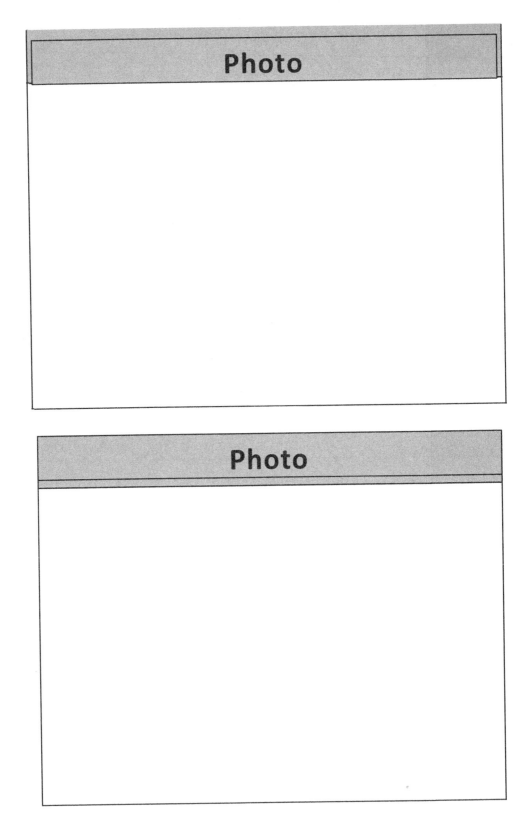

Photo

Photo

Date:	
Weather:	
Season:	
Location:	
Bird Sighting	
Bird Species:	
Time Seen:	
Markings:	
Description	
Notes/Remarks	

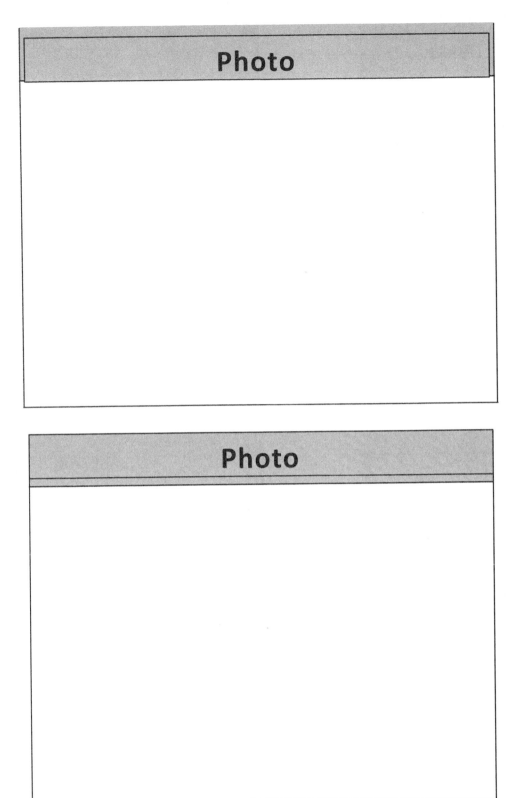

Date:	
Weather:	
Season:	
Location:	

Bird Sighting

Bird Species:	
Time Seen:	
Markings:	

Description

Notes/Remarks

Photo

Photo

Date:	
Weather:	
Season:	
Location:	

Bird Sighting	
Bird Species:	
Time Seen:	
Markings:	

Description

Notes/Remarks

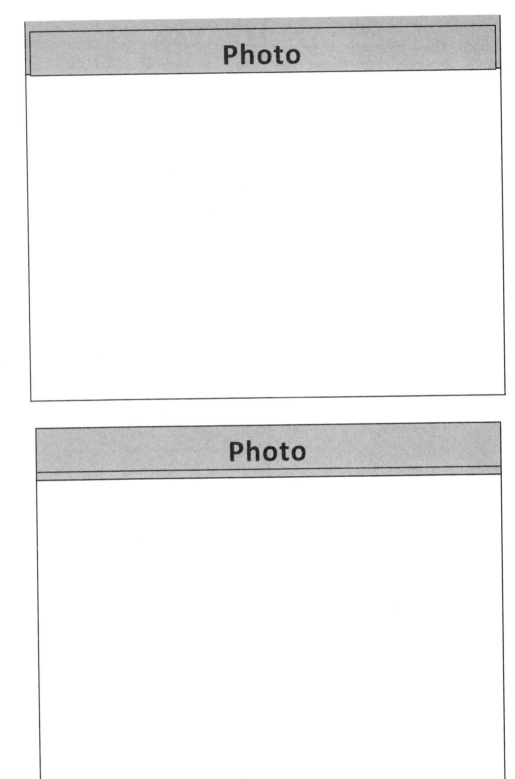

Date:	
Weather:	
Season:	
Location:	

Bird Sighting

Bird Species:	
Time Seen:	
Markings:	

Description

Notes/Remarks

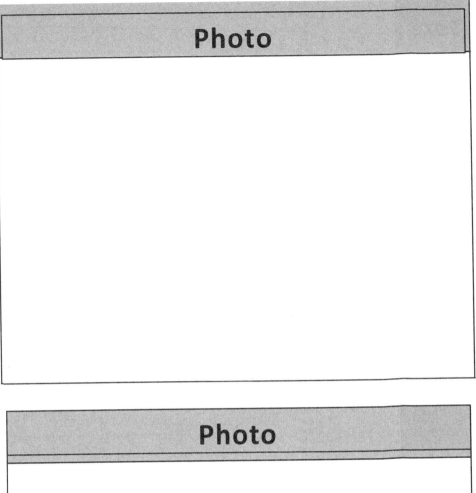

Photo

Photo

Date:	
Weather:	
Season:	
Location:	

Bird Sighting

Bird Species:	
Time Seen:	
Markings:	

Description

Notes/Remarks

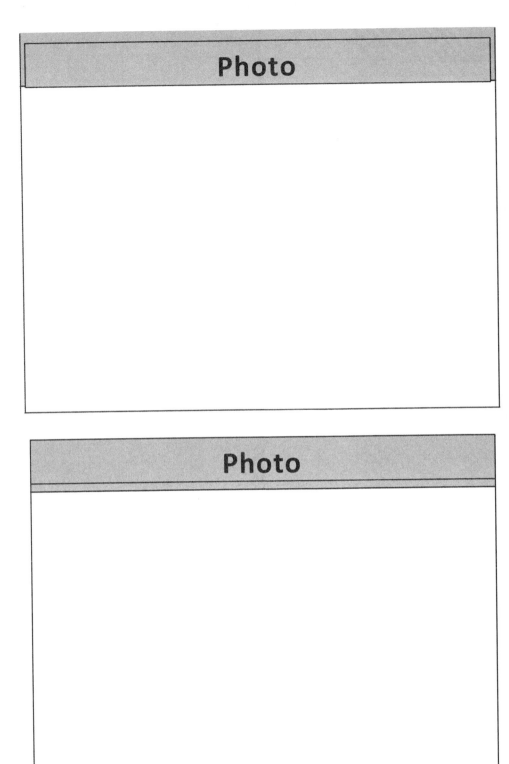

Date:	
Weather:	
Season:	
Location:	

Bird Sighting

Bird Species:	
Time Seen:	
Markings:	

Description

Notes/Remarks

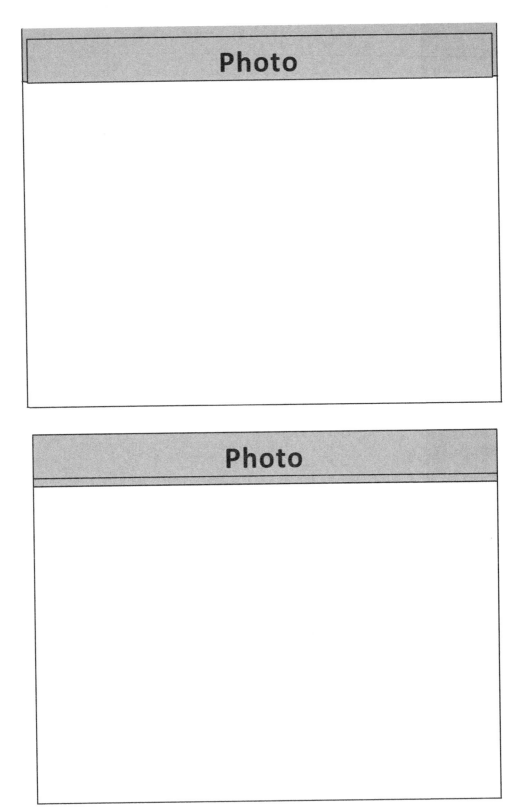

Date:	
Weather:	
Season:	
Location:	

Bird Sighting

Bird Species:	
Time Seen:	
Markings:	

Description

Notes/Remarks

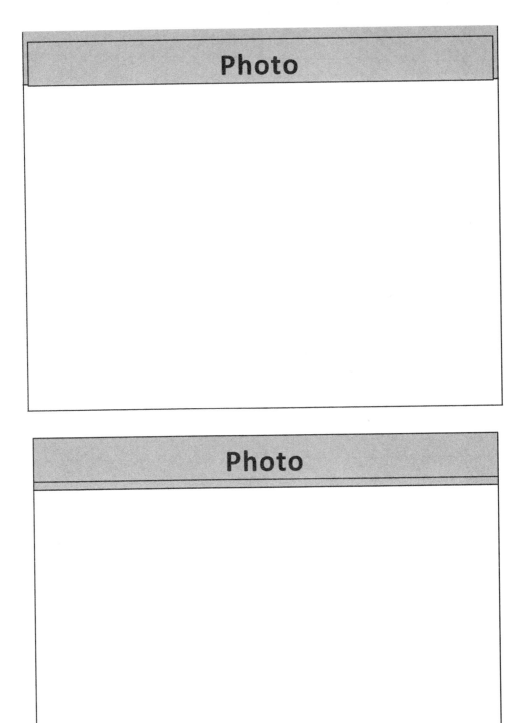

Date:	
Weather:	
Season:	
Location:	

Bird Sighting

Bird Species:	
Time Seen:	
Markings:	

Description

Notes/Remarks

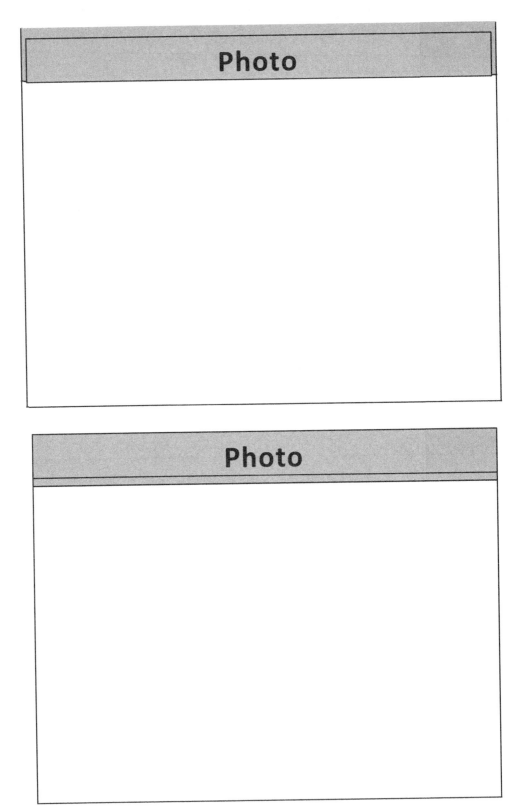

Date:	
Weather:	
Season:	
Location:	

Bird Sighting	
Bird Species:	
Time Seen:	
Markings:	

Description

Notes/Remarks

Photo

Photo

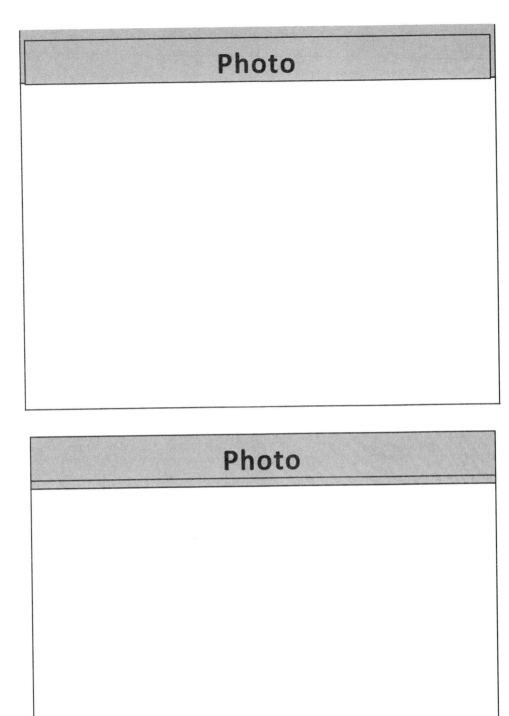

Date:	
Weather:	
Season:	
Location:	

Bird Sighting

Bird Species:	
Time Seen:	
Markings:	

Description

Notes/Remarks

Photo

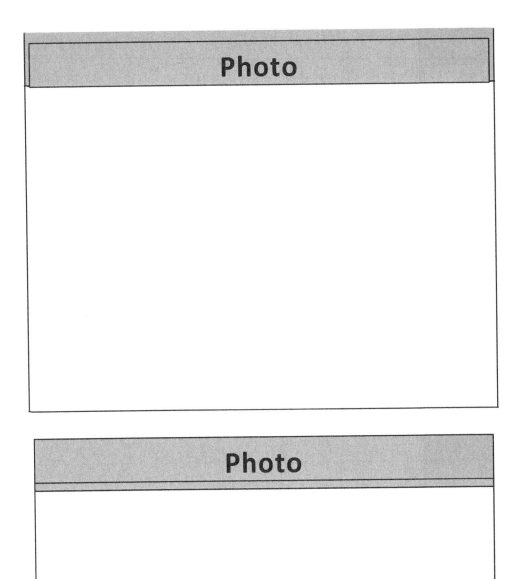

Photo

Date:	
Weather:	
Season:	
Location:	

Bird Sighting

Bird Species:	
Time Seen:	
Markings:	

Description

Notes/Remarks

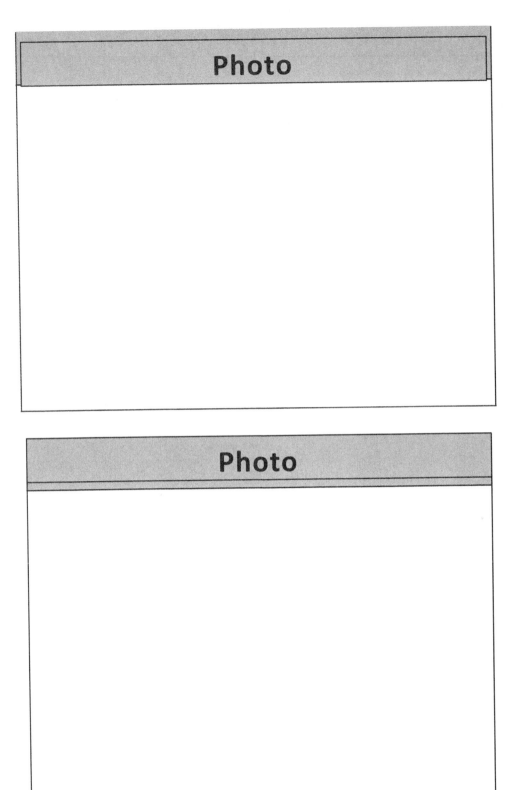

Date:	
Weather:	
Season:	
Location:	

Bird Sighting

Bird Species:	
Time Seen:	
Markings:	

Description

Notes/Remarks

Photo

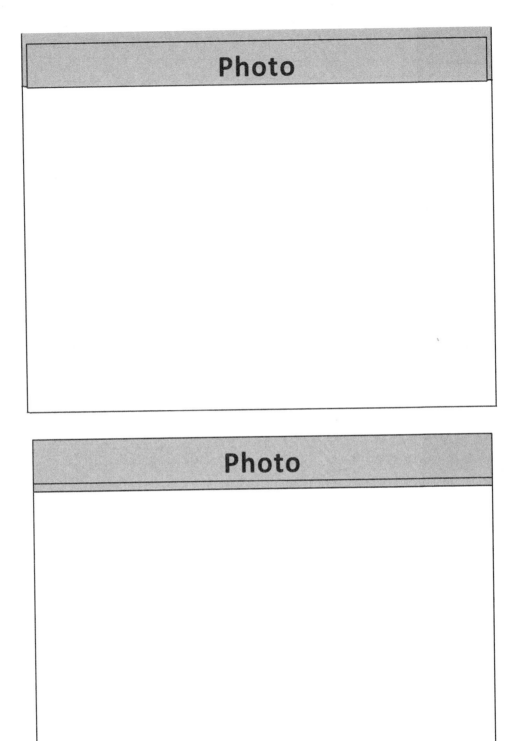

Photo

Date:	
Weather:	
Season:	
Location:	

Bird Sighting

Bird Species:	
Time Seen:	
Markings:	

Description

Notes/Remarks

Photo

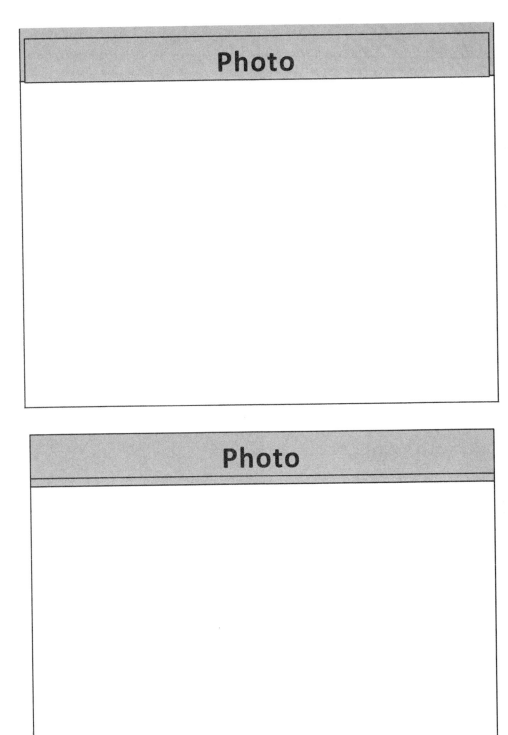

Photo

Date:	
Weather:	
Season:	
Location:	

Bird Sighting	
Bird Species:	
Time Seen:	
Markings:	

Description

Notes/Remarks

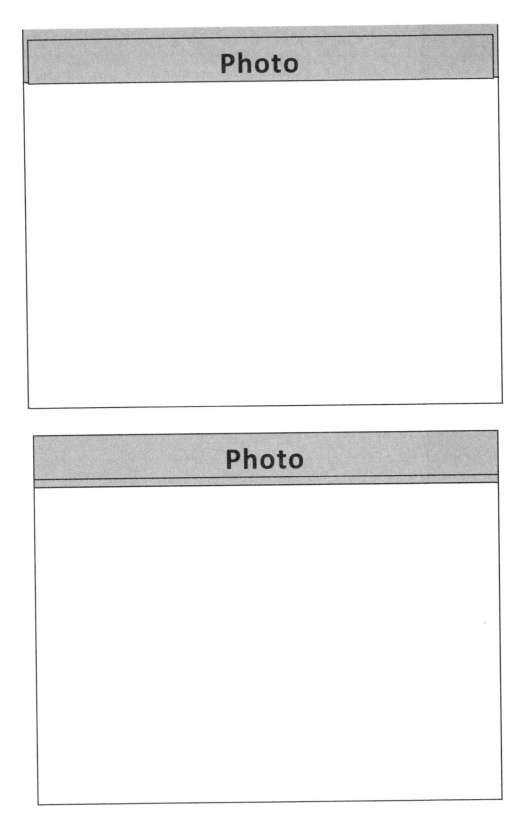

Photo

Photo

Date:	
Weather:	
Season:	
Location:	

Bird Sighting

Bird Species:	
Time Seen:	
Markings:	

Description

Notes/Remarks

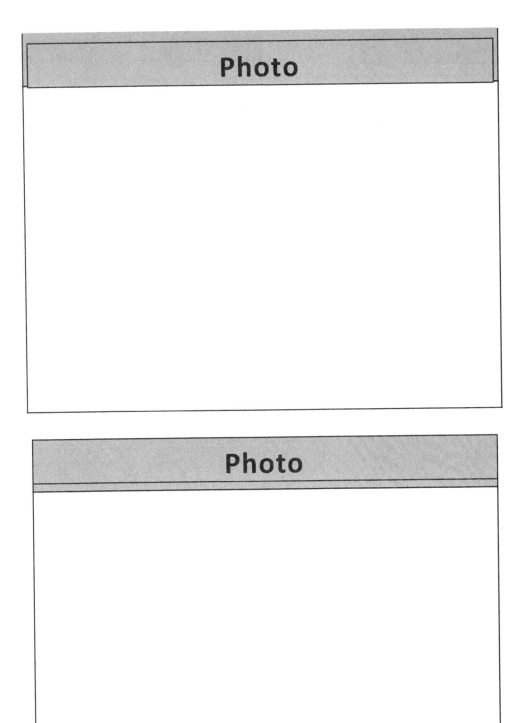

Date:	
Weather:	
Season:	
Location:	

Bird Sighting

Bird Species:	
Time Seen:	
Markings:	

Description

Notes/Remarks

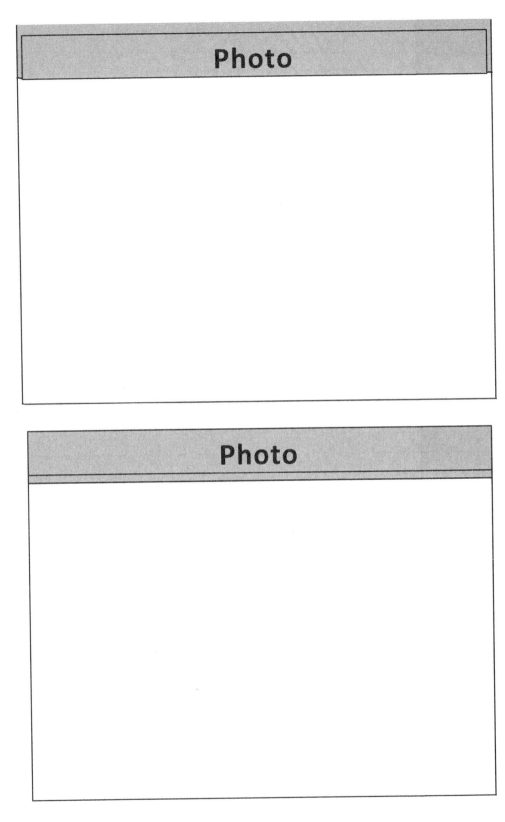

Date:	
Weather:	
Season:	
Location:	

Bird Sighting

Bird Species:	
Time Seen:	
Markings:	

Description

Notes/Remarks

Photo

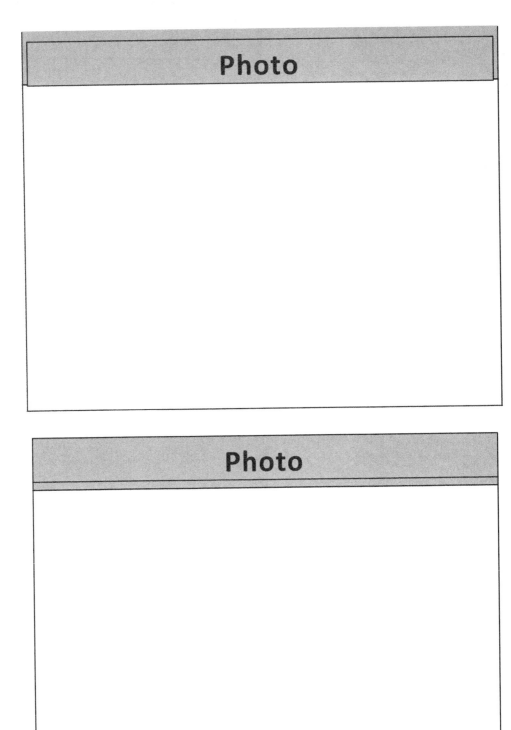

Photo

Date:	
Weather:	
Season:	
Location:	

Bird Sighting

Bird Species:	
Time Seen:	
Markings:	

Description

Notes/Remarks

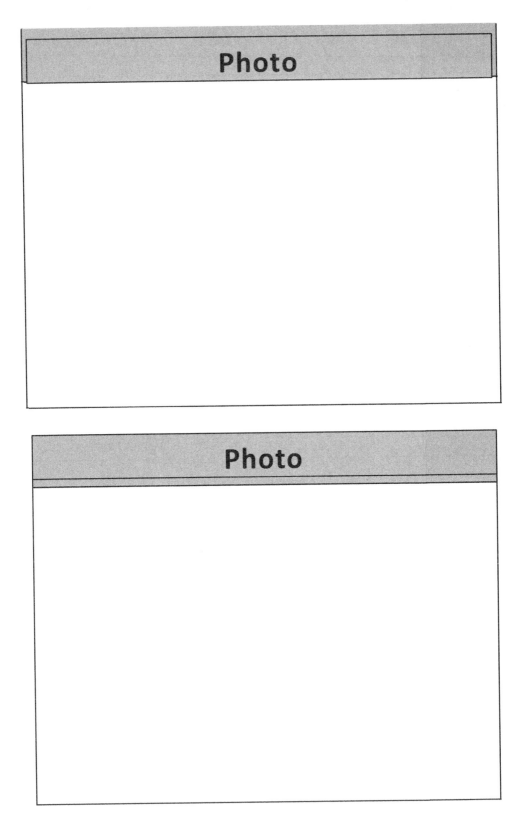

Photo

Photo

Date:	
Weather:	
Season:	
Location:	

Bird Sighting

Bird Species:	
Time Seen:	
Markings:	

Description

Notes/Remarks

Photo

Photo

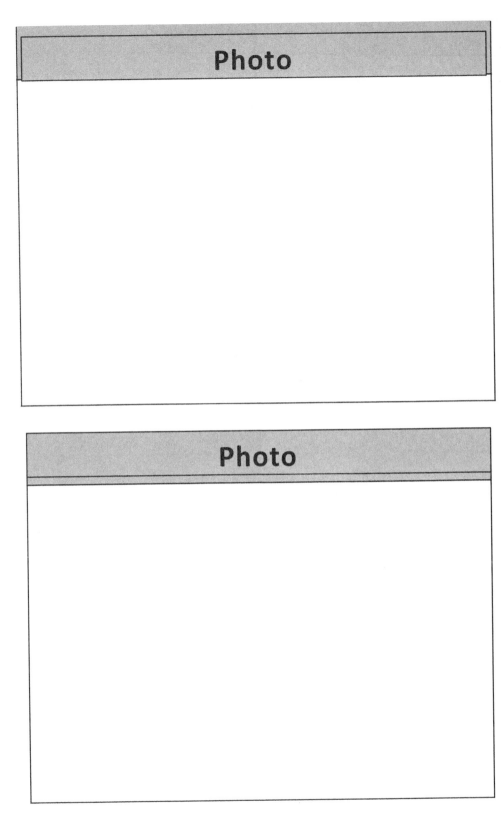

Date:	
Weather:	
Season:	
Location:	

Bird Sighting

Bird Species:	
Time Seen:	
Markings:	

Description

Notes/Remarks

Photo

Photo

Date:	
Weather:	
Season:	
Location:	

Bird Sighting

Bird Species:	
Time Seen:	
Markings:	

Description

Notes/Remarks

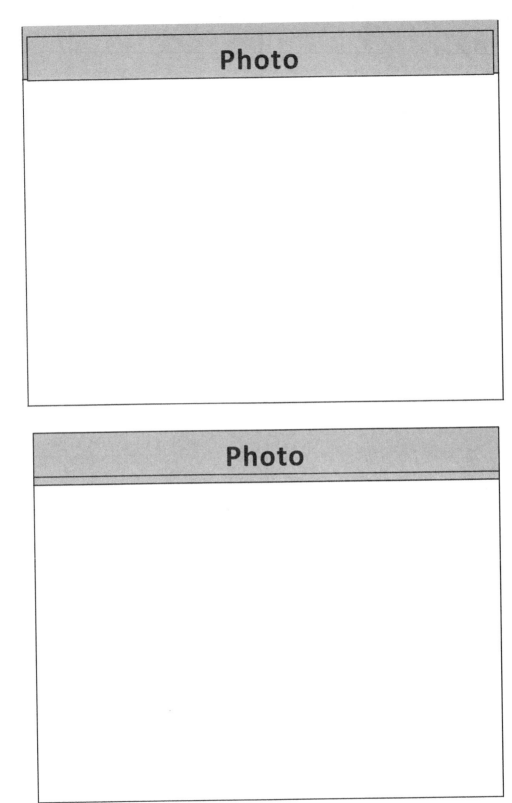

Date:	
Weather:	
Season:	
Location:	

Bird Sighting

Bird Species:	
Time Seen:	
Markings:	

Description

Notes/Remarks

Photo

Photo

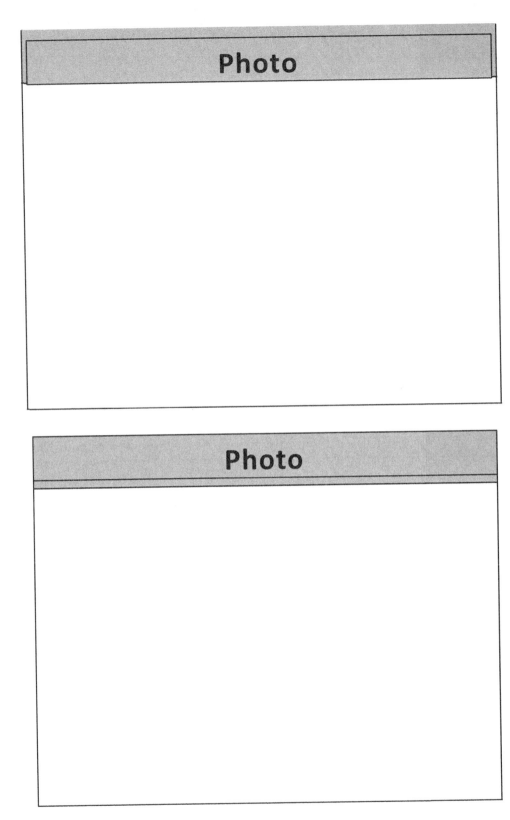

Date:	
Weather:	
Season:	
Location:	

Bird Sighting

Bird Species:	
Time Seen:	
Markings:	

Description

Notes/Remarks

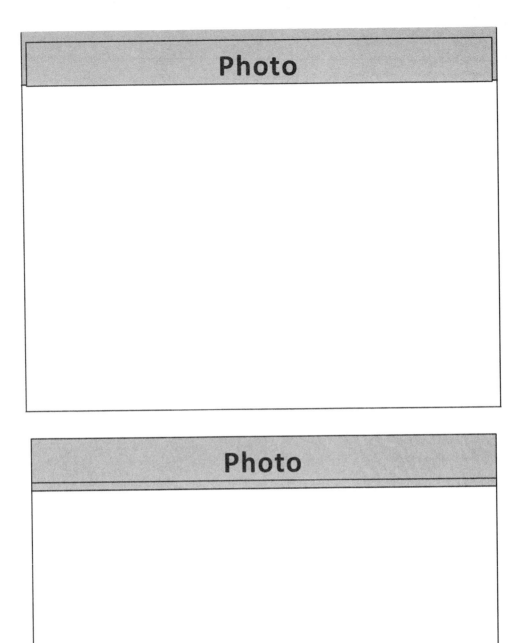

Photo

Photo

Date:	
Weather:	
Season:	
Location:	

Bird Sighting

Bird Species:	
Time Seen:	
Markings:	

Description

Notes/Remarks

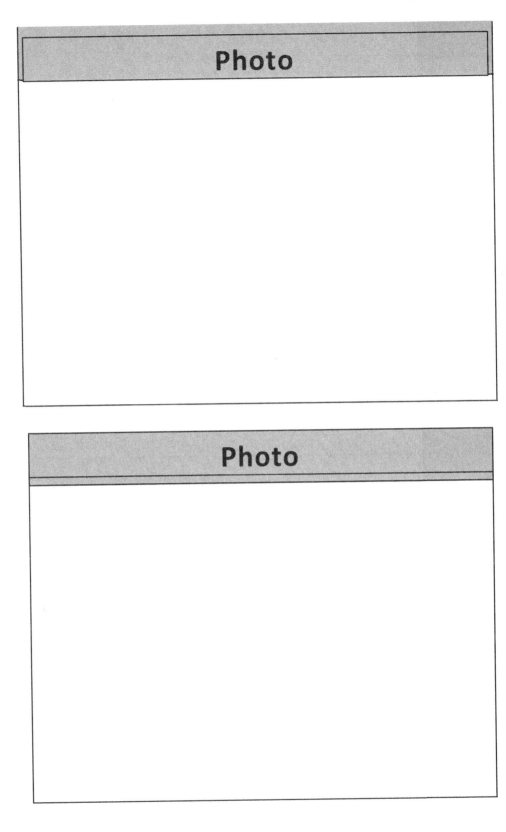

Photo

Photo

Date:	
Weather:	
Season:	
Location:	

Bird Sighting

Bird Species:	
Time Seen:	
Markings:	

Description

Notes/Remarks

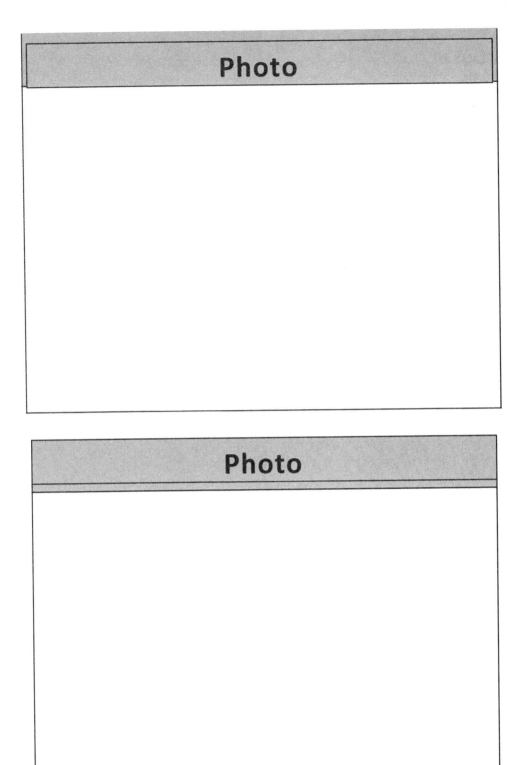

Date:	
Weather:	
Season:	
Location:	

Bird Sighting

Bird Species:	
Time Seen:	
Markings:	

Description

Notes/Remarks

Photo

Photo

Date:	
Weather:	
Season:	
Location:	

Bird Sighting

Bird Species:	
Time Seen:	
Markings:	

Description

Notes/Remarks

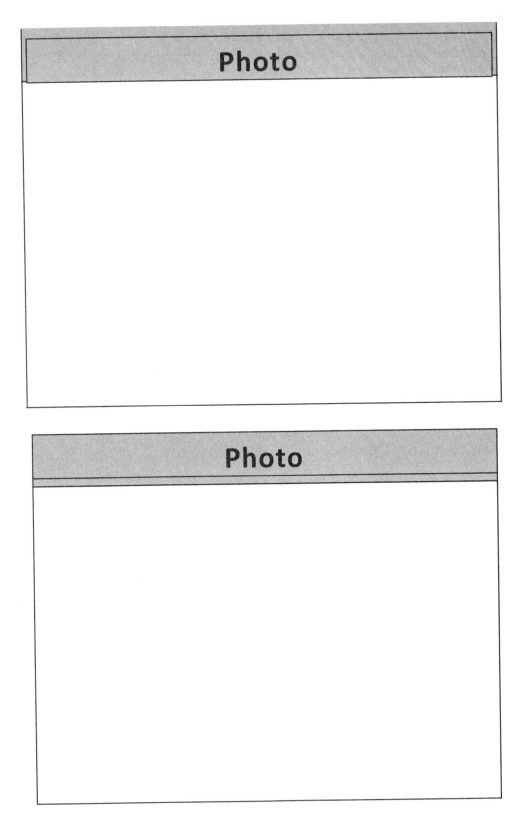

Date:	
Weather:	
Season:	
Location:	

Bird Sighting

Bird Species:	
Time Seen:	
Markings:	

Description

Notes/Remarks

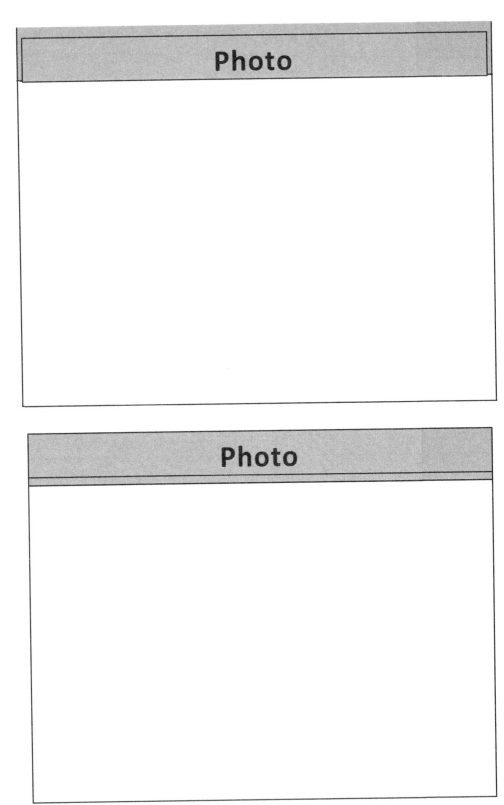

Photo

Photo

Date:	
Weather:	
Season:	
Location:	

Bird Sighting	
Bird Species:	
Time Seen:	
Markings:	

Description

Notes/Remarks

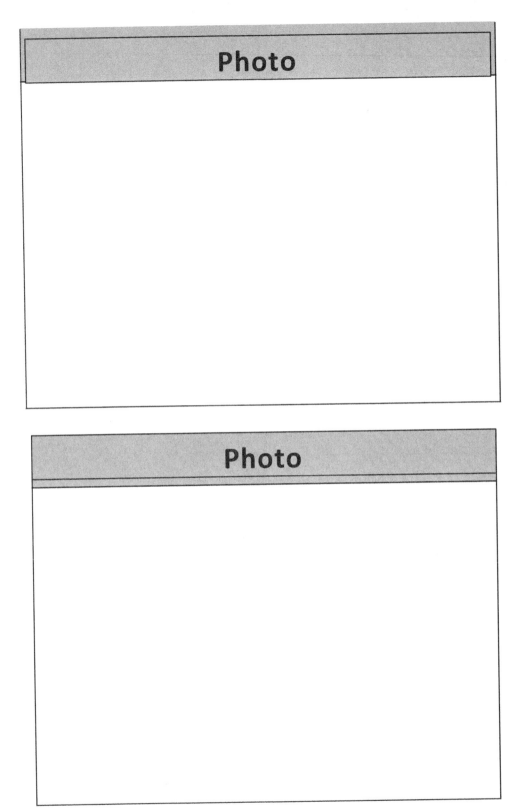

Date:	
Weather:	
Season:	
Location:	

Bird Sighting

Bird Species:	
Time Seen:	
Markings:	

Description

Notes/Remarks

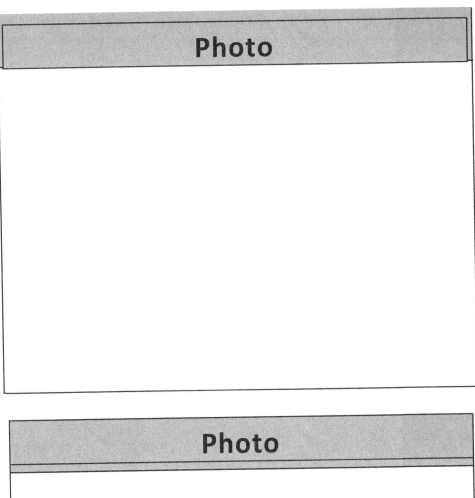

Date:	
Weather:	
Season:	
Location:	

Bird Sighting	
Bird Species:	
Time Seen:	
Markings:	

Description

Notes/Remarks

Photo

Photo

Date:	
Weather:	
Season:	
Location:	

Bird Sighting

Bird Species:	
Time Seen:	
Markings:	

Description

Notes/Remarks

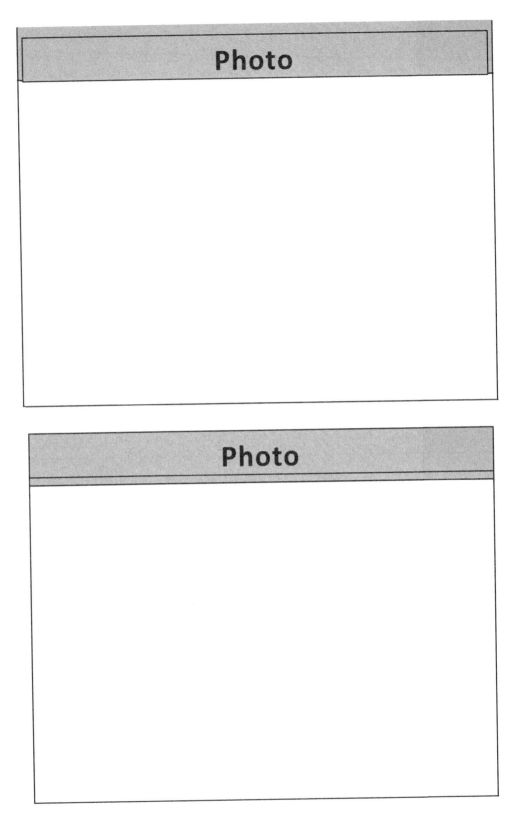

Photo

Photo

Date:	
Weather:	
Season:	
Location:	
Bird Sighting	
Bird Species:	
Time Seen:	
Markings:	
Description	
Notes/Remarks	

Photo

Photo

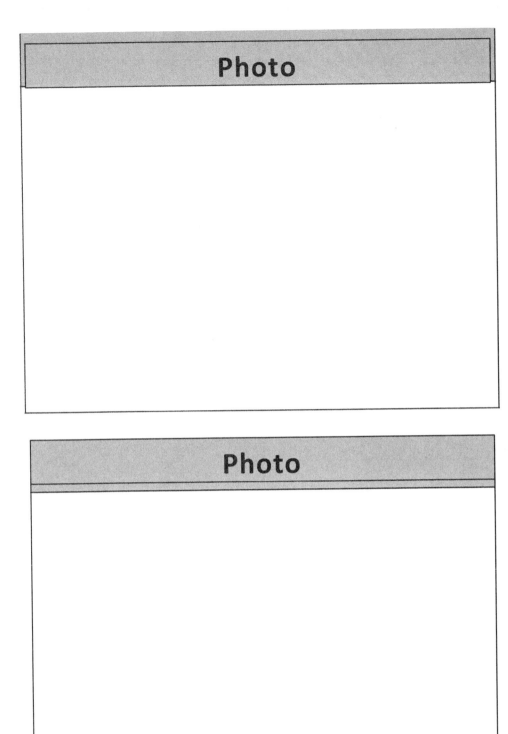

Date:	
Weather:	
Season:	
Location:	

Bird Sighting

Bird Species:	
Time Seen:	
Markings:	

Description

Notes/Remarks

Photo

Photo

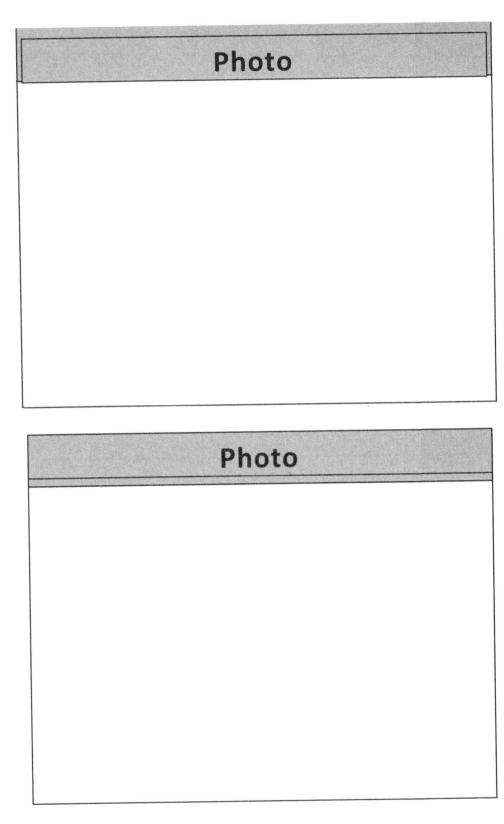

Date:	
Weather:	
Season:	
Location:	

Bird Sighting	
Bird Species:	
Time Seen:	
Markings:	

Description

Notes/Remarks

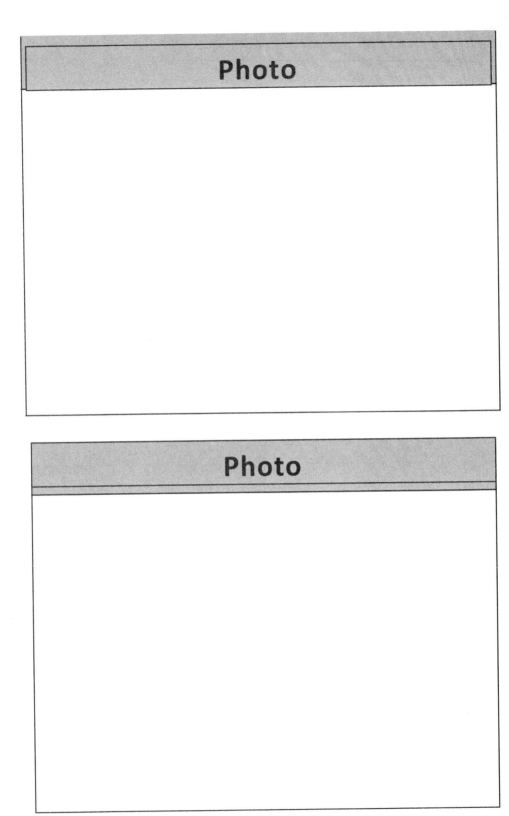

Photo

Photo

Date:	
Weather:	
Season:	
Location:	

Bird Sighting	
Bird Species:	
Time Seen:	
Markings:	

Description

Notes/Remarks

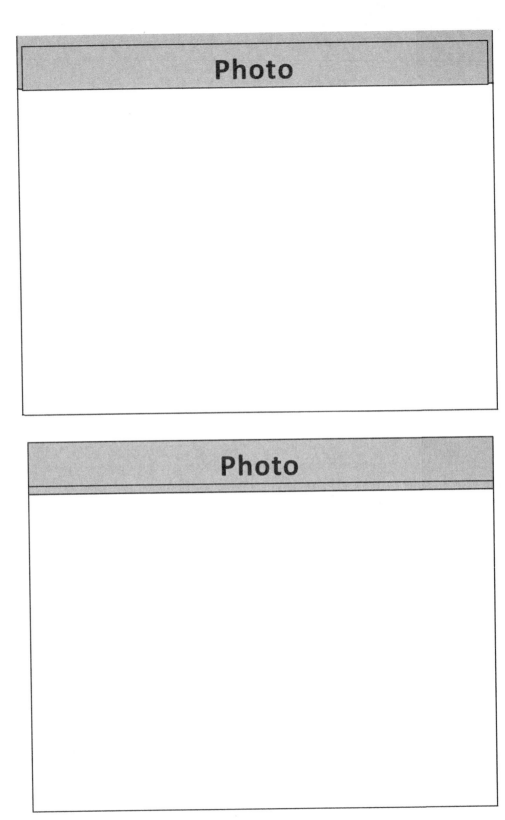

Date:	
Weather:	
Season:	
Location:	

Bird Sighting

Bird Species:	
Time Seen:	
Markings:	

Description

Notes/Remarks

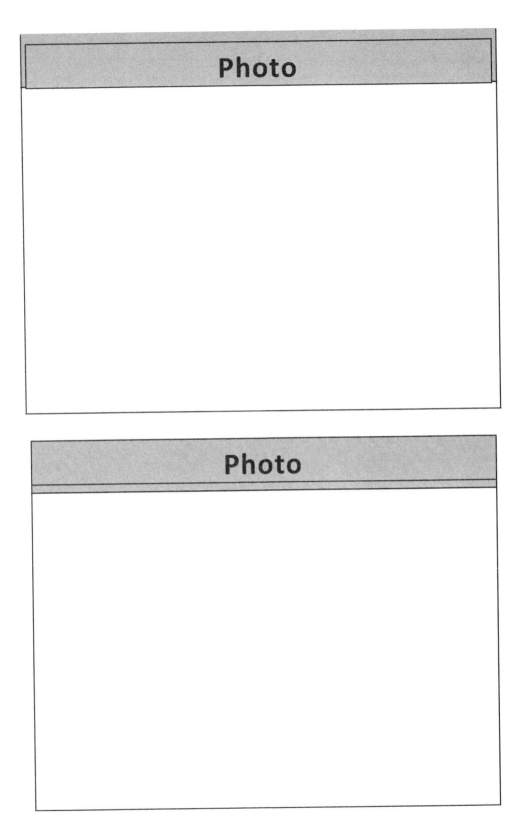

Date:	
Weather:	
Season:	
Location:	

Bird Sighting

Bird Species:	
Time Seen:	
Markings:	

Description

Notes/Remarks

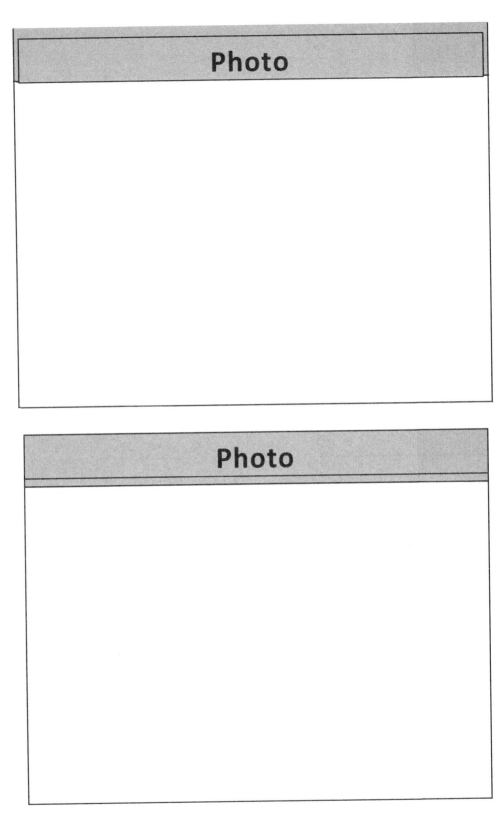

Date:	
Weather:	
Season:	
Location:	

Bird Sighting

Bird Species:	
Time Seen:	
Markings:	

Description

Notes/Remarks

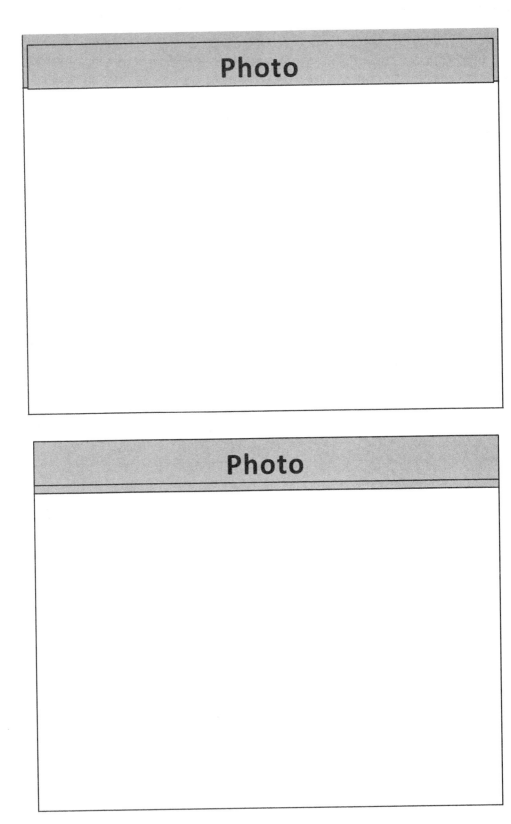

Date:	
Weather:	
Season:	
Location:	
Bird Sighting	
Bird Species:	
Time Seen:	
Markings:	

Description

Notes/Remarks

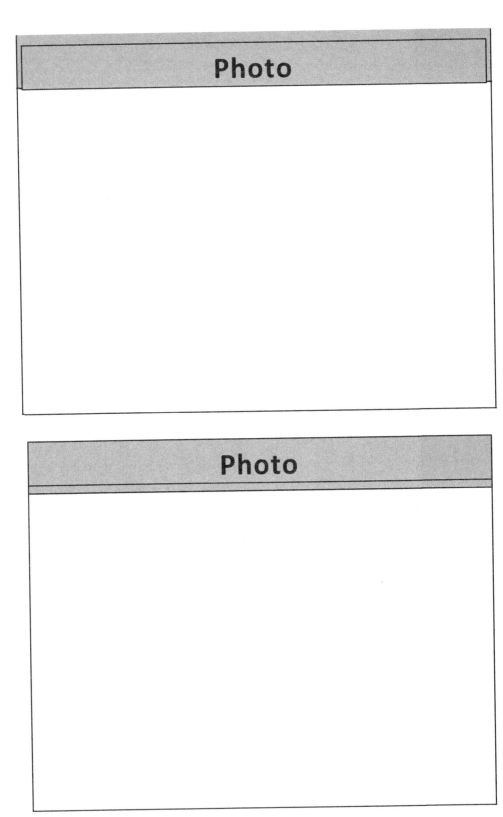

Date:	
Weather:	
Season:	
Location:	

Bird Sighting	
Bird Species:	
Time Seen:	
Markings:	

Description

Notes/Remarks

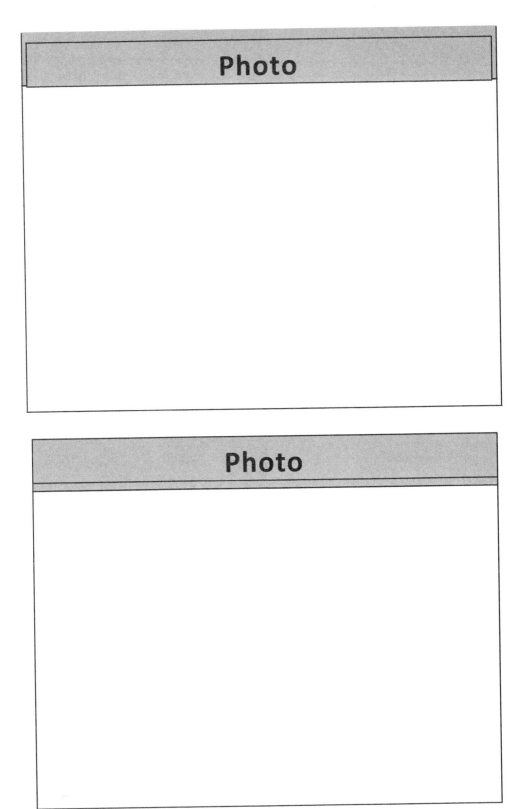

Photo

Photo

Date:	
Weather:	
Season:	
Location:	

Bird Sighting

Bird Species:	
Time Seen:	
Markings:	

Description

Notes/Remarks

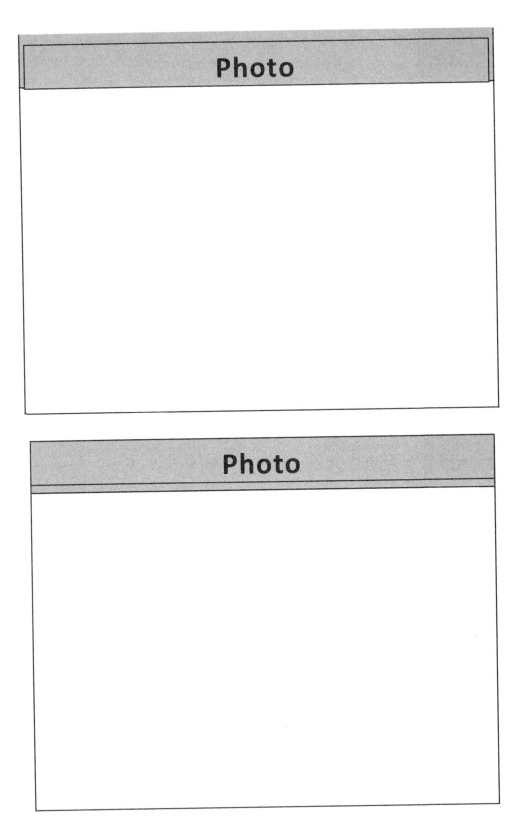

Photo

Photo

Date:	
Weather:	
Season:	
Location:	

Bird Sighting

Bird Species:	
Time Seen:	
Markings:	

Description

Notes/Remarks

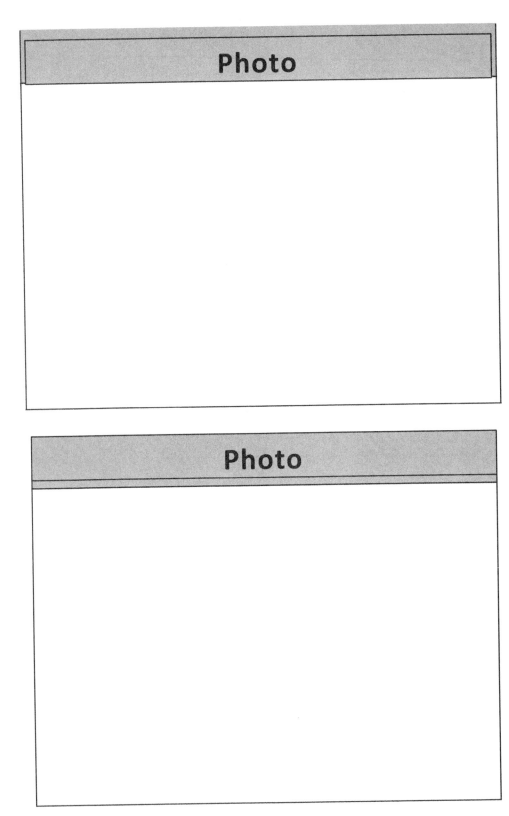

Date:	
Weather:	
Season:	
Location:	

Bird Sighting

Bird Species:	
Time Seen:	
Markings:	

Description

Notes/Remarks

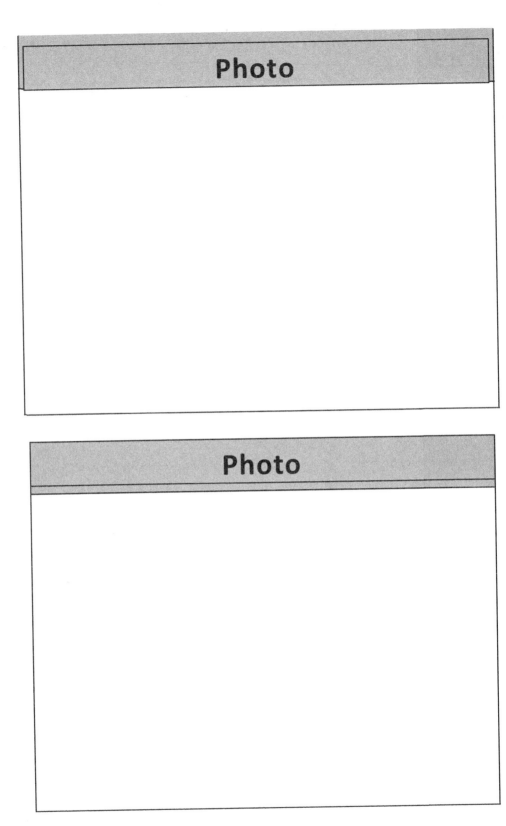

Photo

Photo

Date:	
Weather:	
Season:	
Location:	

Bird Sighting	
Bird Species:	
Time Seen:	
Markings:	

Description

Notes/Remarks

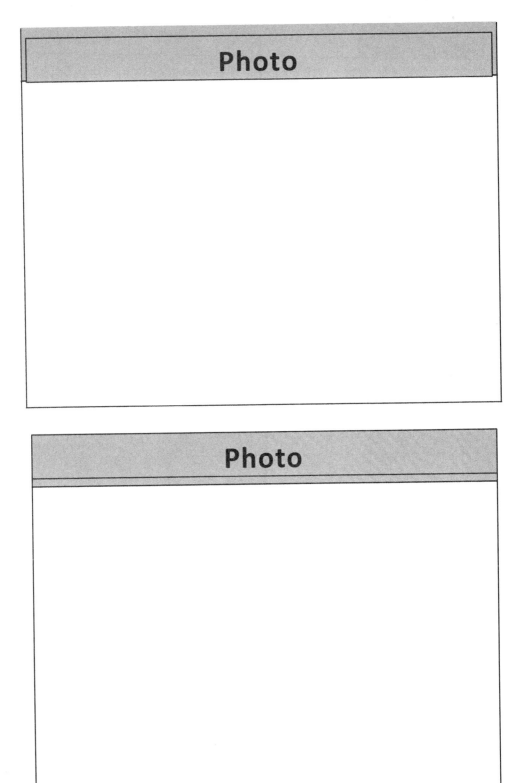

Photo

Photo

Date:	
Weather:	
Season:	
Location:	

Bird Sighting

Bird Species:	
Time Seen:	
Markings:	

Description

Notes/Remarks

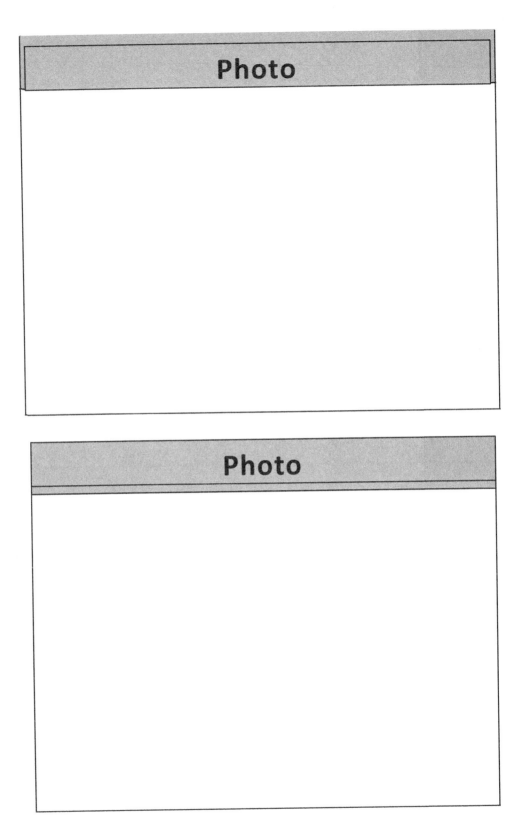

Date:	
Weather:	
Season:	
Location:	

Bird Sighting

Bird Species:	
Time Seen:	
Markings:	

Description

Notes/Remarks

Photo

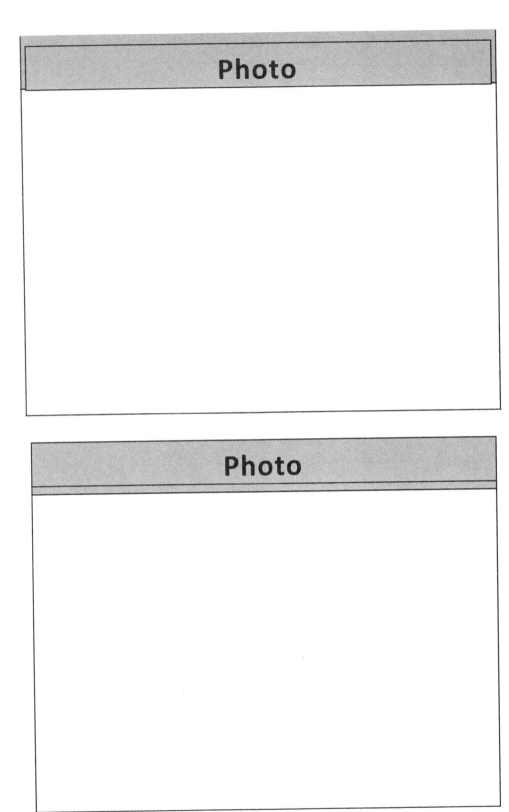

Photo

Date:	
Weather:	
Season:	
Location:	

Bird Sighting	
Bird Species:	
Time Seen:	
Markings:	

Description

Notes/Remarks

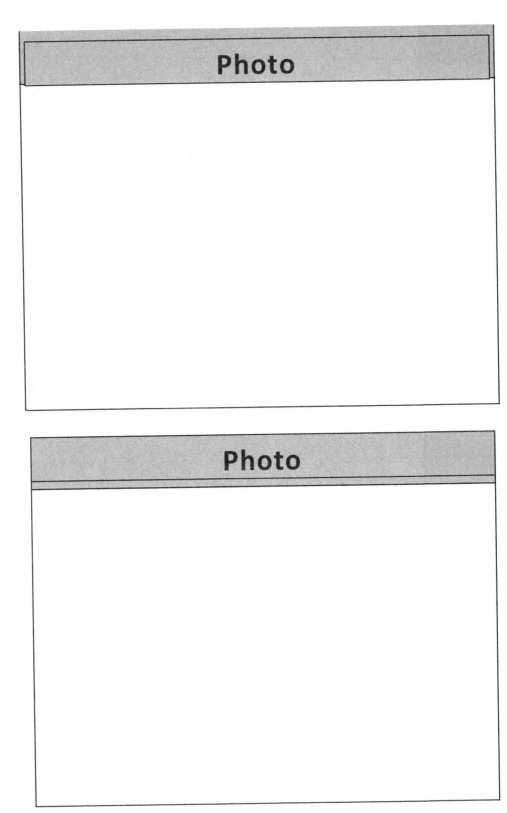

Photo

Photo

Date:	
Weather:	
Season:	
Location:	

Bird Sighting

Bird Species:	
Time Seen:	
Markings:	

Description

Notes/Remarks

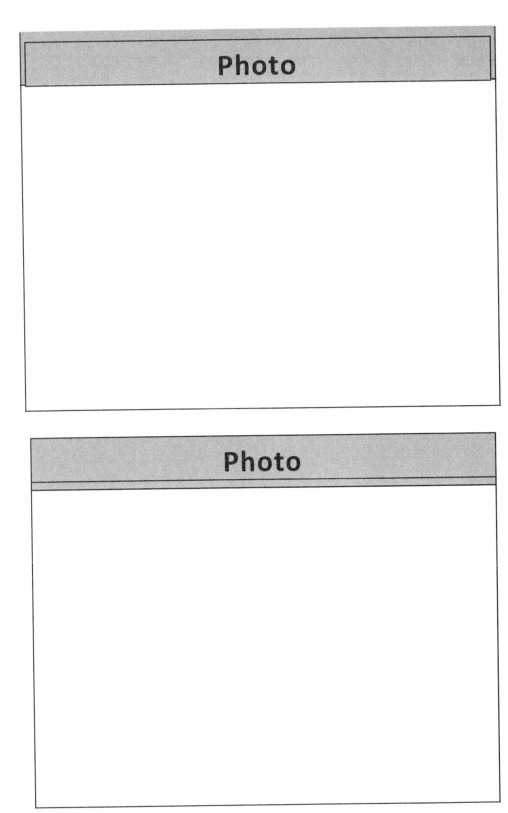

Photo

Photo

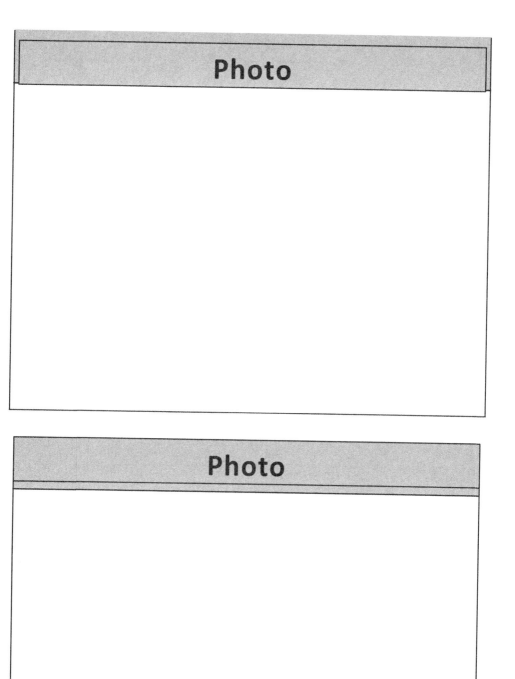

Photo

Photo

Photo

Photo

Photo

Photo

PROS
AND CONS

MAKE BETTER LIFE
CHOICES EVERY DAY!

Van Life
LIVING THE
DREAM!

Notes From The Road
Less Traveled

PARADOX PRESS

Printed in Great Britain
by Amazon

25374970R00071